This book belongs to

Couleur
Color

Blanc
White

Rouge
Red

Vert
Green

Jaune
Yellow

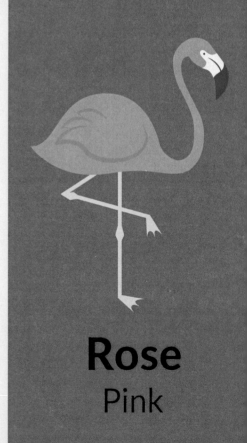

Rose
Pink

Gris
Grey

Bleu
Blue

Orange
Orange

Violet
Purple

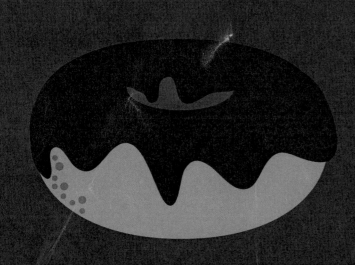

Marron
Brown

Noir
Black

Forme
Shape

Rectangle
Rectangle

Triangle
Triangle

Cœur
Heart

Cercle
Circle

Ovale
Oval

Carré
Square

Étoile
Star

Chiffre
Figure

Un
One

Deux
Two

Trois
Three

Quatre
Four

Cinq
Five

Six
Six

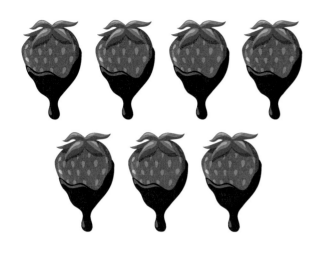

Sept
Seven

Huit
Eight

Neuf
Nine

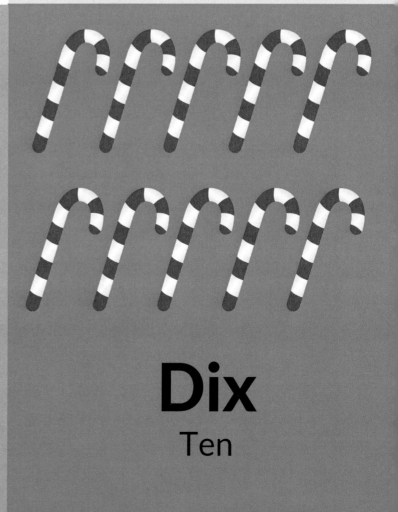

Dix
Ten

Famille
Family

Père
Father

Mère
Mother

Fils
Son

Fille
Daughter

Bébé
Baby

Frère

Brother

Sœur

Sister

Grand-père

Grandfather

Grand-mère

Grandmother

Corps
Body

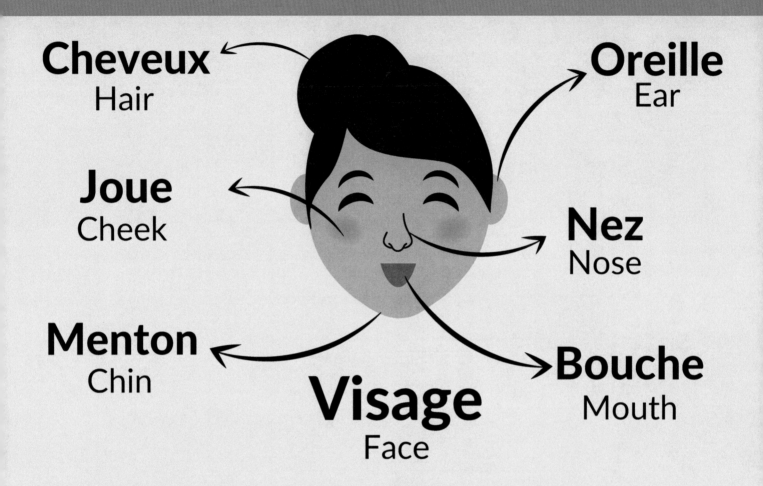

Cheveux
Hair

Oreille
Ear

Joue
Cheek

Nez
Nose

Menton
Chin

Bouche
Mouth

Visage
Face

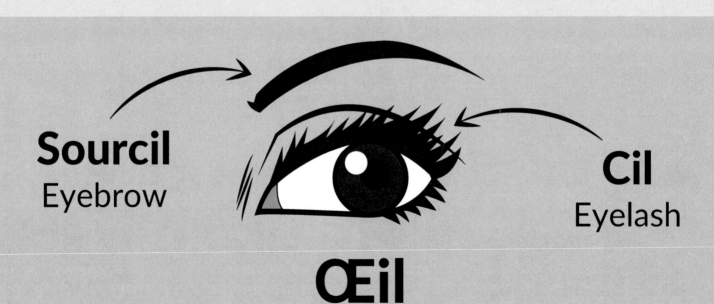

Sourcil
Eyebrow

Cil
Eyelash

Œil
Eye

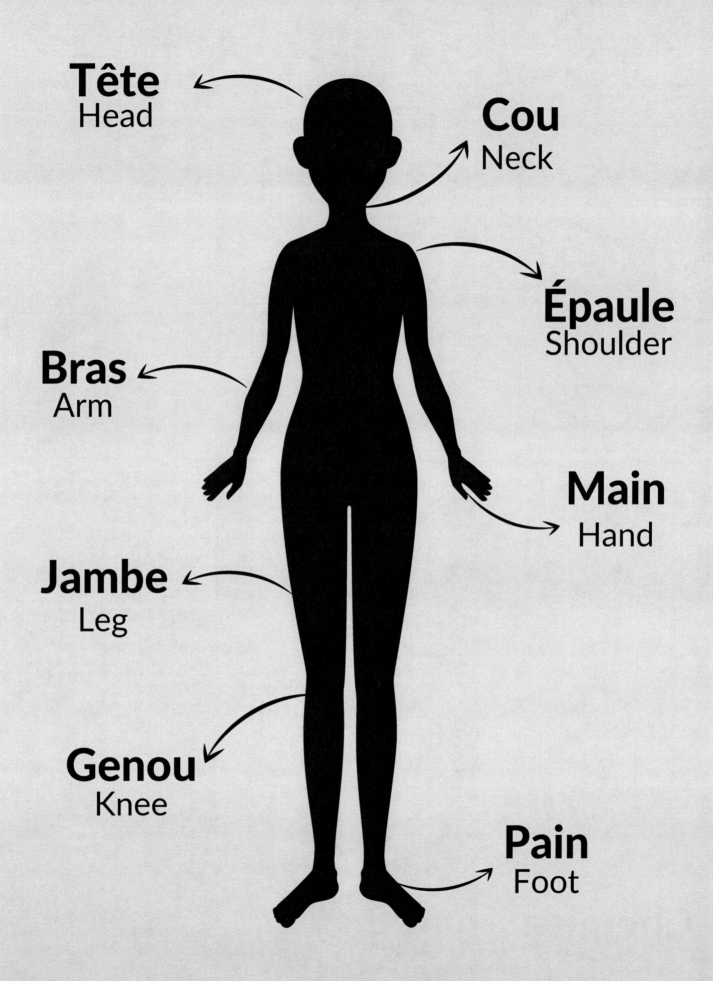

Tête
Head

Cou
Neck

Épaule
Shoulder

Bras
Arm

Main
Hand

Jambe
Leg

Genou
Knee

Pain
Foot

Vêtement
Clothing

Pantalon
Trousers

Jupe
Skirt

Robe
Dress

Chemise
Shirt

Pull
Sweater

Manteau
Coat

Cravate
Tie

Chaussette
Sock

Chaussure
Shoe

Chapeau
Hat

Gant
Glove

Écharpe
Scarf

Maison
Home

Fauteuil
Armchair

Chaise
Chair

Porte
Door

Fenêtre
Window

Canapé
Sofa

Coussin
Pillow

Baignoire
Bathtub

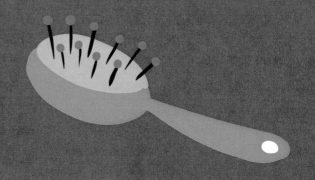

Brosse à cheveux
Hairbrush

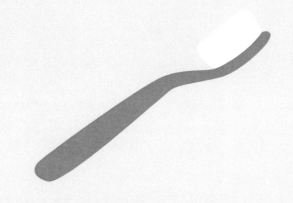

Brosse à dents
Toothbrush

Dentifrice
Toothpaste

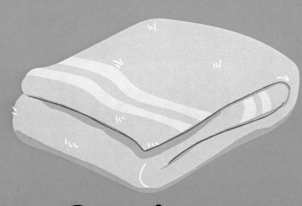

Serviette
Towel

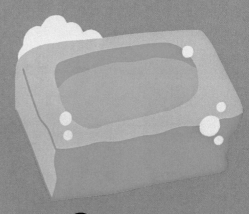

Savon
Soap

Animal
Animal

Chien
Dog

Chat
Cat

Lapin
Rabbit

Cheval
Horse

Poule
Hen

Mouton
Sheep

Canard
Duck

Singe
Monkey

Vache
Cow

Ours
Bear

Escargot
Snail

Oiseau
Bird

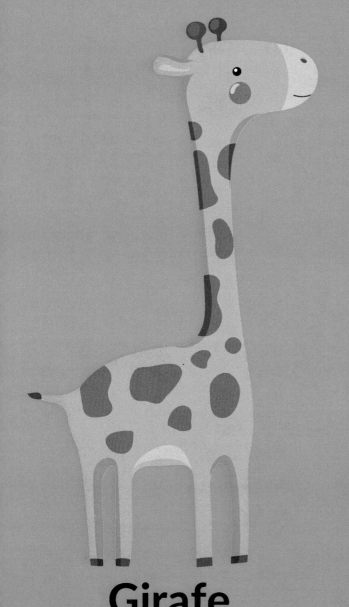

Girafe
Giraffe

Éléphant
Elephant

Poisson
Fish

Nature
Nature

Soleil
Sun

Lune
Moon

Nuage
Cloud

Ciel
Sky

Pluie
Rain

Jour

Day

Nuit

Night

Neige
Snow

Feuille
Leaf

Fleur
Flower

Tempête
Thunderstorm

Arbre
Tree

Transport
Transportation

Bateau
Boat

Moto
Motorbike

Bicyclette
Bicycle

Voiture
Car

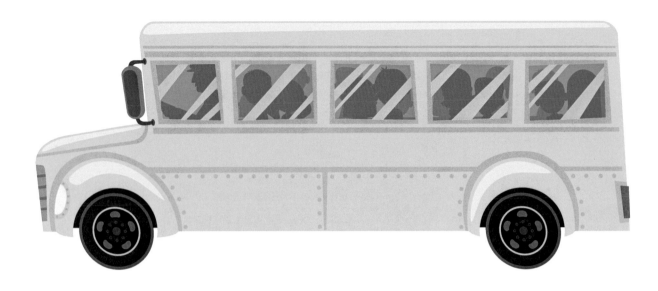

Bus
Bus

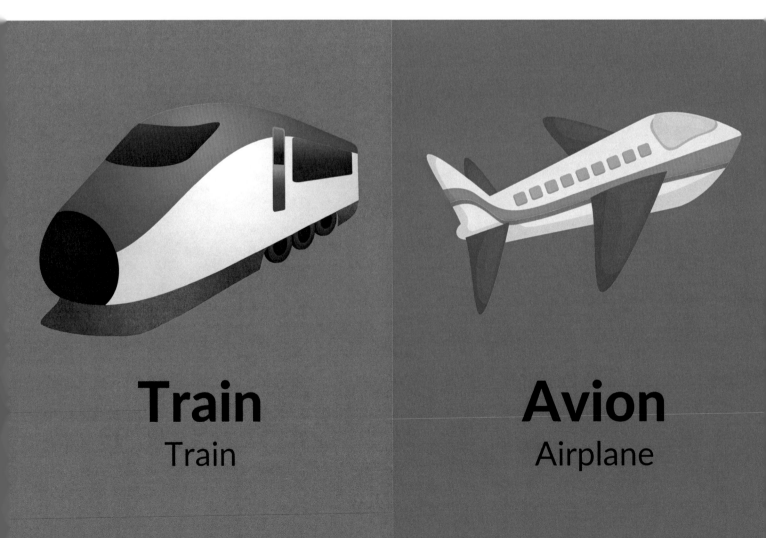

Train
Train

Avion
Airplane

Nourriture
Food

Riz
Rice

Huile
Oil

Pain
Bread

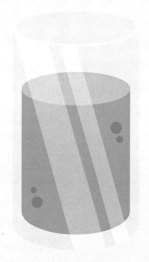

Eau
Water

Lait
Milk

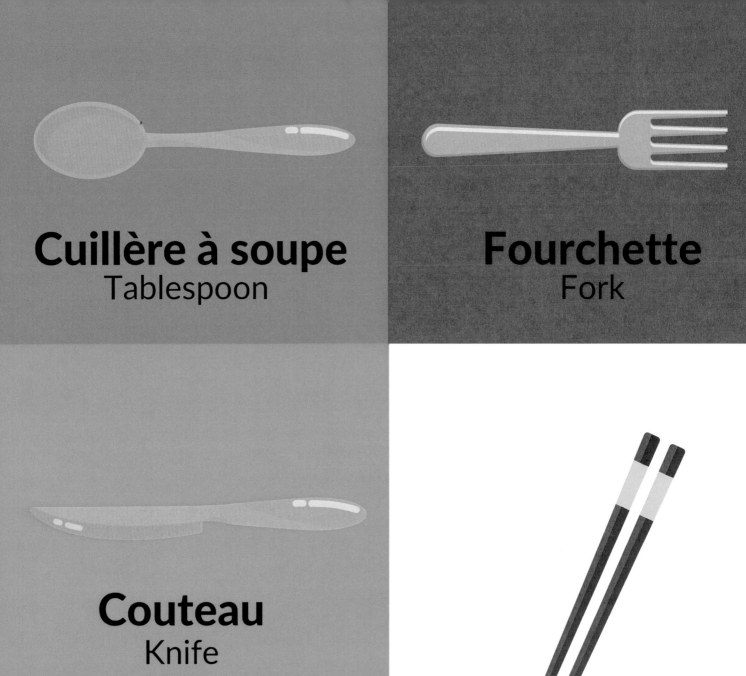

Cuillère à soupe
Tablespoon

Fourchette
Fork

Couteau
Knife

Cuillère à café
Teaspoon

Baguettes
Chopsticks

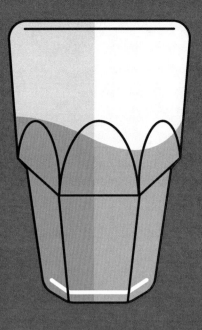

Verre
Glass

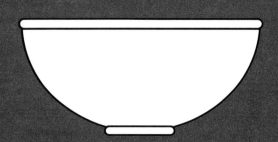

Bol
Bowl

Assiette
Plate

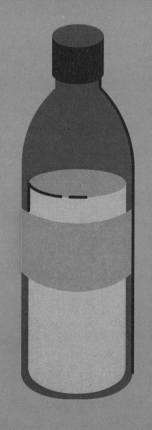

Bouteille
Bottle

Tasse
Cup

Fruit / Légume
Fruit / Vegetable

Banane
Banana

Citron
Lemon

Pomme
Apple

Fraise
Strawberry

Pastèque
Watermelon

Poireau
Leek

Citrouille
Pumpkin

Tomate
Tomato

Carotte
Carrot

Oignon
Onion

Métier
Job

Pompier
Fireman

Docteur
Doctor

Agriculteur
Farmer

Cuisinier
Cook

Policier
Police officer

Professeur
Teacher

Chanteur
Singer

Avocat
Lawyer

Infirmier
Nurse

Saison
Season

Printemps
Spring

Été
Summer

Hiver
Winter

Automne
Fall / Autumn

Sport
Sport

Volleyball
Volleyball

Équitation
Horse riding

Course à pied
Running

Tennis
Tennis

Football
Football (UK), Soccer

Plongée
Diving

Basketball
Basketball

Musculation
Bodybuilding

NOTES

NOTES

NOTES

NOTES

NOTES